First Day
and
Football Surprise

Level 0 – Lilac

©2020 **BookLife Publishing Ltd.**
King's Lynn, Norfolk PE30 4LS

ISBN 978-1-83927-005-5

All rights reserved. Printed in Malaysia.
A catalogue record for this book is available from the British Library.

First Day & Football Surprise
Story by Gemma McMullen
Illustrated by Andrew Heather

An Introduction to BookLife Readers...

Our Readers have been specifically created in line with the London Institute of Education's approach to book banding and are phonetically decodable and ordered to support each phase of the Letters and Sounds document.

Each book has been created to provide the best possible reading and learning experience. Our aim is to share our love of books with children, providing both emerging readers and prolific page-turners with beautiful books that are guaranteed to provoke interest and learning, regardless of ability.

BOOK BAND GRADED using the Institute of Education's approach to levelling.

PHONETICALLY DECODABLE supporting each phase of Letters and Sounds.

EXERCISES AND QUESTIONS to offer reinforcement and to ascertain comprehension.

BEAUTIFULLY ILLUSTRATED to inspire and provoke engagement, providing a variety of styles for the reader to enjoy whilst reading through the series.

AUTHOR INSIGHT:
GEMMA MCMULLEN

Gemma McMullen is one of BookLife Publishing's most multi-faceted and talented individuals. Born in Newport, Gwent, she studied at the University of Northampton, where she graduated with a BA (Hons) in English and Drama. She then attended the University of Wales where she obtained her PGCE Primary qualification, and has been teaching ever since. Her experience as a teacher enables her to find exactly what makes children focus and learn, and allows her to write books that amuse and fascinate their readers.

This book focuses on inspiring imagination and interest. This is a lilac level 0 book band.

First Day

Story by
Gemma McMullen

Illustrated by
Andrew Heather

Football Surprise

story by Gemma McMullen

Illustrated by Andrew Heather

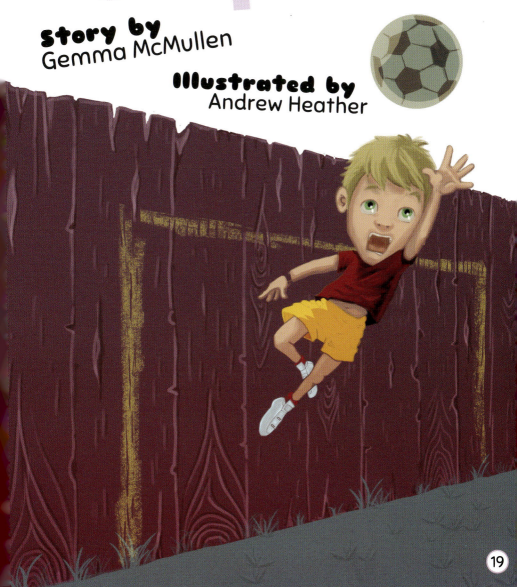